Overcome

secret sins

in

15 Days

M.J. Welcome

Smart Publishing House
Division of MDW Consulting Group
Far Rockaway, NY 11691
www.smartpublishinghouse.com

Dwain G. Welcome, **Editor**

First Published by Smart House Publishing 01/15/2015

ISBN-13: 978-0692368992
ISBN-10: 069236899X

Printed in the United States of America

Note: This publication is intended to provide helpful information on the subject matter covered. It is sold with the understanding that the author and publisher are not rendering professional services in the book. If the reader requires personal or spiritual advice, a competent professional should be consulted.

Contents

ACKNOWLEDGEMENTS

I would like to thank God for the opportunity to write this devotional and for His favor in getting it published. I bless the Lord for my family who supported, proofread and edited the manuscript. May the Lord bless you for your love, support and encouragement!

A special thanks goes to John, a member of the Fellowship of Christian Writers critique group (FCW) for your willingness to critique and give valued suggestions and insights. May the Lord continue to bless you as you write, critique and edit to advance the Kingdom of God.

INTRODUCTION

Greetings in the name of Jehovah!

I'm glad you decided to take action to address to your secret sin(s). We all have sins that we would rather keep hidden from prying eyes or wagging tongues. At some point in our lives, we all have tried to avoid shame by putting forth a polished image, hidden behind the veil of half-truths. Or we may have done things we thought were justifiable at the time but were actually deemed sins in the sight of God.

This book does not dwell on the sin, but rather focuses on God's simple remedy for sin. Our goal is to overcome secret sins by exposing it to the Light. In order to expose it, we need to become aware of the strategies the enemy uses to ensnare and tempt us to walk in the shadows. If we submit to God and resist the temptation to compromise (to become dim lights,) the enemy will flee from us (James 4:7).

However, if we fall into evil (sin) the way out is through repentance and confession. As believers, we're called to weed sin, out of our lives. We are to lay hold of ourselves and judge sin, as sin. We are not to rationalize, reason, cast blame, deny, hide, or justify wrongdoing.

Those who refuse to acknowledge their sin will eventually have to stand before the Lamb on the Day of Judgment. If we follow God's mandate to repent and confess our sins we'll secure our place in the light of his presence. If we refuse, we have chosen to be children of disobedience traveling along the path of darkness and not the way of light through Christ Jesus.

In this *15-day devotional*, we will examine *15 Bible verses* on Secret Sins. We'll learn how God views secret sins, His prescribed course of action and we'll discover if there truly is something called hidden sins in the sight of God. In addition, we'll learn how to become aware of our secret sins and how to expose them to the Light of Christ.

Each devotional is based on the Hebrew or Greek interpretation of the scripture. The daily activities give you the opportunity to search the Word and gain deeper understanding of God's Word. We use the Strong's Concordance references which are also online at http://blueleterbible.org to search out the deeper truths of God's Word by examining their root meanings. All scriptures are from the King James Version (KJV) of the Bible.

If you're committed to living the life God intended for you from the very foundation of the world, then by faith seize this opportunity to be cleansed.

Here's to *your* **VICTORY** over *secret sins*!

M.J. Welcome

A*s a believer...* I promise to:

- ✓ Examine myself in truth
  (2 Corinthians 13:5)
- ✓ Be prepared to confess my sins
  (1 John 1:9)
- ✓ Refuse to justify, rationalize or excuse
  my wrongs
  (John 15:22 and Romans 2:1)
- ✓ I will pray by faith for hidden things
  to be expose to the Light of Christ
  Jesus (Ephesians 5:13)
- ✓ I will judge myself as Christ would
  judge me (1 Corinthians 2:15)
- ✓ I will turn from wrongdoing
  (Job 33:15-18)
- ✓ I will not be ashamed (Psalms 25:3
  and Isaiah 54:4)
- ✓ I will not walk with condemnation
  (Romans 8:1)
- ✓ I will love myself because God loves
  me (Mark 12:31 and 1 John 4:8)

GOD SHALL BRING EVERY WORK INTO JUDGMENT

"For God shall bring every work into judgment, with every secret thing, whether it be good, or whether it be evil."

—Ecclesiastes 12:14

Judgment, a concept that many believers have difficulty with today. Hating to judge and hating to be judged.

God the Father, Christ the Son and Holy Spirit however are all about judgment. They judge everything. As spiritual beings they examine everything, judging it good or evil, pleasant (higher nature) or unpleasant (lower nature), ethically right or ethically wicked.

Everything is analyzed, acts, deeds, pursuits, accomplishments, celebrations, and how we raise and teach our children. God judges the things we produce, the work that we do (of deliverance and judgment), the things we undertake, and the things that we acquire (like our property). How we order lives (home, and things we do etc.), our achievements, the things we offer, things we prepare, or institute, the things we use, our enterprises, and our businesses are all subject to God's judgments.

Each one of us will be brought before Christ, the judge on the Day of Judgment. He will review our case or cause. He will make a decision based on the law, God's law, and not man's law. Not according to political correctness, popular opinion or the latest trend or fad. Not based on what the great thinkers of the day have concluded. But solely based on God the Father's righteous ordinances found in His Word.

Secret things… hidden sins … concealed things will be exposed to the light. So will shameful deeds, self-serving lies, depraved acts, and perverse thoughts. All will be exposed.

What will testify against us? It will be ourselves!

Every idle word we have spoken throughout our lives will speak out against us. They will be called out and mentioned by name and we will have to give an account.

> *"But I say unto you, That every idle word that men shall speak, they shall give account thereof in the day of judgment."*
> —Matthew 12:36

Thankfully, Christ is not an unjust or partial judge. Our good deeds will also be brought forth for judgment. Every ethical decision, right action, living according to our higher spiritual nature, acts of kindness, and delightfulness will testify for us.

Christ will determine whether we are fit for the kingdom. He will measure out to each of us the proper reward, whether punishment or vindication, condemnation or acceptance (Matthew 16:27, Job 34:11).

> *"Who will render to every man according to his deeds:"*
> —Romans 2:6

> *"And, behold, I come quickly; and my reward is with me, to give every man according as his work shall be."*
> —Revelation 22:12

Will we be sentenced or welcomed in?

His decision will be final. There will be no court of appeal. No long waiting time on judgment row, hoping for the decision to be overturned. When the verdict is rendered it will be immediate and swiftly carried out.

While there is time, let us seek to do well, to operate in our higher nature after the pattern of Jesus. For as spiritual sons we are able to judge all things as our Father does. We can discern between good and evil and choose the good as our brother Jesus did. And we can live, walk, act, and speak according to what we hear as Holy Spirit leads us.

"But he that is spiritual judges all things, yet he himself is judged of no man."
—1 Corinthians 2:15

"For as many as are led by the Spirit of God, they are the sons of God."
—Romans 8:14

DAY 1

SECRET SINS EXPOSED

As you read today's devotional did Holy Spirit reveal to you an area where you have sinned? An area where you are harboring a secret sin? It's time for you to judge. Will hiding it help you to be more unified with God or will it produce fruits of division from God? Is it good or evil?

If Holy Spirit has identified the sin by name so should you! If He judges it evil so should you. God requires us to come into the light as He did with Adam and Eve (Genesis 3:8-10) only then can He give us new garments (Genesis 3:21). Only God can remove the filth of shame and guilt from us.

This is your opportunity to expose *your* secret sins to the light thus increasing your brightness before the God of light (2 Corinthians 3:18). Are you ready?

PRAYER

Dear Lord,

Thank you for your Word and for helping me to learn about your ways. Father, I ask you to expose every secret thing in my life. It's my desire to do what is right, pleasant and pleasing to you. Help me to learn your ways of judgment. Help me to apply it to my life in obedience starting today. This I pray in Jesus name. Amen

ACTIVITY

The Word of God tells us in 2 Timothy 2:15, to *"Study to shew thyself approved unto God, a workman that needeth not to be ashamed, rightly dividing the word of truth.*"

The following activity is to encourage you to go deeper, seek harder, and learn more about the Word of truth. The scripture below has the Strong Concordance reference numbers beside them. When you look up the numbers, you'll learn the Hebrew or Greek word and in some cases, you'll find their base meaning in other root words. As you dig down to the primary root word, you'll discover the enormity of what God addresses in each word of each scripture.

It may take you time to complete it all but when you do, you'll never view scripture the same again. You will know that there is more to it than what you have heard, learned or believed. This is God's way of causing his children to mature. It's for those who are able to eat meat.

> *"I have fed you with milk, and not with solid food: for until now you were not able to bear it, neither yet now are you able."*
> —1 Corinthians 3:2

Let us take a closer look at our devotional scripture:

> *For God* H430 *shall bring* H935 *every work* H4639 *into judgment,* H4941 *with every secret thing,* H5956 *whether it be good,* H2896 *or whether it be evil.* H7451
> —Ecclesiastes 12:14

In order grasp what's communicated in the scripture we have to dissect each word to get the true meaning. Let's examine the first word in the verse with the Strong's reference number H430.

When we look up the number in the Strong's Concordance we see it is the word *Elohiym* which has several meanings one if which is rulers or judges. The root word (etymology) comes from *Elowahh* Hebrew reference H433 which means God or false god.

As we dig down further we see that the root meaning comes from the word *El* H410 which means god-like one, mighty one, mighty heroes among other things. This word comes from a root meaning from the word *Ayil* H352 which means ram (food, sacrifice, skin dyed red, for tabernacle). As we continue we find that, the root meaning of *Ayil* comes from *Uwl* H193 which means prominence, wealthy men, belly or body (contemptuous).

Continue to look up each word writing out the meaning in a study notebook and at the end, put it all together with the aid of Holy Spirit to grasp the fullness of God's message to you. If you don't have a concordance use the one online at www.blueletterbible.org. Type in the verse in the search box. Click on the Strong's tab on the bar below the search bar (it is located between copy options and red-letter this works for the KJV only).

If you want to go even further you can read the Genius' Hebrew-Chaldee Lexicon which is located on each page for each word. Just scroll down on the page and you will see it. Click to read the complete entry. If you desire to see other verses that use the same word, continue to scroll down the page.

Now that you know what to do, it is up to you to invest the time and energy to search the scriptures and unearth deeper understanding. Hidden in them are treasures beyond measure. As you search, God *will* ensure that you find truth (Matthew 7:7-8, Luke 11:9, Jeremiah 29:13).

Day 2

SECRETS SINS IN THE LIGHT

*"Thou hast set our iniquities before thee, our
secret **sins** in the light of thy countenance."*
—Psalms 90:8

Many of us have guarded secrets. Things that we believe no one else knows. It could be foolish acts we did when we were zealous and ignorant (1 Timothy 1:13) things done when we were unbelievers (Psalms 78:22). Or things we did in our youth. It may even be sins we still commit under the cloak of darkness or in the shadows after we become believers.

Psalms 90:8, tells us clearly that our depravity, perversity, and guilt are set before God. The way we distort the image of God by our behavior, choices, or sin are clearly in His view. What we believe are concealed and hidden sins, are not hidden at all. They are visible before our omniscient God. They are illuminated in his presence.

Our sins are in front of his face in the light of his presence and for this, we should be thankful.

When our sins are before Him, we still have an opportunity to turn away from perversity and back toward righteousness. When God is still paying attention to our behavior we have a chance to be straightened like a palm tree.

If God turns, his face from us (Isaiah 59:2) would we be able to see the light? Would we be able to find our way in the dark?

No! Sin is *only* exposed by the light of God's righteousness as revealed through the law of God and the righteousness of Christ Jesus (Galatians 3:19, Romans 7:7-25, and Romans 3:21).

DAY 2

SECRET SINS EXPOSED

As believers our hearts desires should mirror those of our Father God. Our place of habitation should reflect his habitation. God exists in pure light. He wants us to be children of light worthy of existing in his presence for eternity (1 Thessalonians 5:5, Ephesians 5:8, and Ephesians 4:17-32). In order to be assured of a place in the light of his presence we have to weed out every sprout of darkness. Fortunately, for us God makes it easy for us to do so, through Jesus Christ.

PRAYER

Dear Lord,

Help me to live in the light of your presence at all times. Open my eyes to see areas where darkness exists. Open my ears to hear the voice of Your Spirit. Give me the strength and courage to do what is right and to exist in the light of Jesus, separated from darkness. Amen.

ACTIVITY

Now that you know how to dissect scripture, take time to review today's devotional verse.

Thou hast set <u>H7896</u> our iniquities <u>H5771</u> before thee, our secret <u>H5956</u> sins in the light <u>H3974</u> of thy countenance. <u>H6440</u>

—Psalms 90:8

DAY 3

CAST OFF THE WORKS OF DARKNESS

"The night is far spent, the day is at hand: let us therefore cast off the works of darkness, and let us put on the armour of light."
—Romans 13:12

It is the duty of *every* believers to emit light in a dark world. It's a sad testimony when light bearers spread, promote and advance the kingdom of darkness. In Romans 13:12, Paul gives sound counsel to believers. He advises us to cast off the works of darkness. Why does he admonish believers to do this? Why tell us what we should already know?

When we are born-again, we enter into a process of being made new. It doesn't happen immediately and it requires commitment and resolve to stay the course. Each day we recommit ourselves to this grueling process of shedding the old nature to put on the new. Some things may come easy, while others pose more of a challenge for us. A battle rages within us. We may do what we don't want to do, and fail to do what we desire to do (Romans 7:15-17).

But why did Paul issue such a strong alarm? Night symbolizes a time when work ceases, but it also represents a time for moral stupidity, for deeds of sin and shame, and for darkness to spread and become thick. Paul lets us know that sin, shame and moral stupidity has been lengthened out or beat out as a smith hammers metal making it longer. This violent advancement of darkness signals its opposition and distinction from God's the natural order of things (Matthew 11:12).

In contrast, an immovable definite day (time) light (righteousness) has been firmly set or appointed for the Great Day of their Wrath (Revelation 6:17). It's as sure as the seasons come and go according to natural law. But he tells us that it is being brought nearer, it is approaching and will soon come to squeeze, throttle, and bend the arm of dark night. It approaches with violence.

Therefore, since this is the case he counsels us to separate ourselves from darkness, sin, shame, and moral stupidity.

Flee from it. Depart from it. Refuse to carry it. Choose not to wear it. Don't spend time with it. Choose not to be in its company. Issue a decree of hatred for darkness. Lay it aside for destruction. Why should we follow his counsel?

Darkness has a plan. Its desire is to cause us to walk in shadows, for our eyes to be darkened, and to cause us not to see the road of destruction ahead of us. In order to avoid the trap we must be willing to change our clothing. Turn our direction. Put distance between us and it by time and location. We have to be willing to clear out our inner areas so that Christ can fully dwell within us.

Our new outfits are weapons of our warfare (Ephesians 6). They are the tools we use in order to bring forth our Father's kingdom; this is the work we are to actively pursue. Our armor of light accomplishes many tasks, it exposes darkness for what it is, and reveals hidden things. Furthermore, it brings forth light, enabling things to come clearly into view, and allows things to grow. Our weapons burns like fire, and shines as a lamp to illuminate our path, and it's a star that helps to guide the way in which we should go (Psalms

119:105, Isaiah 48:17, Psalms 32:8, Isaiah 42:16 and Matthew 2:-12).

The day fast approaches. It's time to cast off the works of darkness and securely put on the armor of light. Let's follow Paul's lifesaving counsel and cast off the works of darkness!

DAY 3

SECRET SINS EXPOSED

As believers we're responsible for working out our salvation (deliverance, safety and preservation) with fear and trembling according to Philippians 2:12. This is an impossible task without divine help.

At times, it can be overwhelming, confusing, frustrating, and aggravating. Yet God expects us to continue the course He has laid out for us, the same course that Jesus completed. Our duty is to fulfill the purpose of God for our lives by overcoming and eradicating darkness where we find it.

PRAYER

Dear Lord,

Thank you for hearing me when I pray (John 11:42 and 1 John 5:14-15). Thank you for your love. Lord I desire to take off the filthy garments of darkness and put on Your robes of light (Zechariah 3:4 and Genesis 35:2). Help me to keep my eyes focused on things above, ever mindful that you have made me more than a conquer through Christ Jesus (Romans 8:31-39).

ACTIVITY

Take a few minutes to examine today's devotional verse more in depth.

The night ^{G3571} is far spent, ^{G4298} ^{G1161} the day ^{G2250} is at hand: ^{G1448} let us ^{G659} ^{G0}

therefore ^{G3767} *cast off* ^{G659} *the works* ^{G2041} *of darkness,* ^{G4655} *and* ^{G2532} *let us put on* ^{G1746} *the armour* ^{G3696} *of light.* ^{G5457}
—Romans 13:12

DAY 4

NO COVER FOR REBELLION

"He that covereth his sins shall not prosper:
but whoso confesseth and forsaketh them shall
have mercy."
—Proverbs 28:13

In our world today, many believe that confession is an archaic endeavor. It's something that our grandparents may have believed but it isn't relevant in our modern and advanced times. But is this line of thinking correct? Is it Biblical?

Proverbs 28:13 tells us, that the individual who covers up his rebellion, revolt, or sin will not experience prosperity, progress, or success. Of course, worldly evidence could be cited to the contrary. There are politicians who have covered their actions (sins) to remain in office. There are clergy who have kept silent and are preaching and teaching weekly. There are school officials and doctors who remain silent in the midst of their wrongdoing, and they perform their duties as if nothing is amiss.

Is staying in office, making money or holding on to a job prospering? Is preserving ones reputation at the cost of one's soul God's idea of success? (Matthew 16:26).

Success is possessing the moral character of Jesus. It's the ability to throw off, cast out, or shoot down wrong doing. It's the willingness to lay hands on oneself with your power and strength and declare yourself guilty of wrongdoing and turn from that wayward course.

When we confess and forsake our rebellion, we are promised mercy, which is God's tender and compassionate love. By throwing down our sinful ways, we are correcting our walk before God and He will love us deeply for following in His way.

> *"The LORD hath appeared of old unto me, saying, Yea, I have loved thee with an everlasting love: therefore with lovingkindness have I drawn thee."*
> —Jeremiah 31:3

DAY 4

SECRET SINS EXPOSED

Existing in the light of God means exposure! There's no room or place for concealed sins. Our minds need to be in sync with the mind of God. When Adam and Eve went and hid themselves under the covering of bushes God called to them (Genesis 3:9). They had to make a choice to step into the light. Daily we are called to make the same choice.

Are we going to confess our sins? Are we willing to turn away from our sins? If we are not then can we truly call ourselves Sons of God?

PRAYER

Dear Lord,

This day I choose to step fully into the light. I desire to forsake all secret sins. Please reveal to me the better choice in every situation, so that my life will be pleasing unto you (Colossians 1:10, Romans 12:2, and 1 Thessalonians 4). I pray, amen.

ACTIVITY

Make an investment today in your future. Examine Proverbs 28:13, under the lens of your microscope and expose any secret sins.

He that covereth <u>H3680</u> his sins <u>H6588</u> shall not prosper: <u>H6743</u> but whoso confesseth <u>H3034</u> and forsaketh <u>H5800</u> them shall have mercy. <u>H7355</u>
—Proverbs 28:13

DAY 5

NO FELLOWSHIP WITH WORKS OF DARKNESS

"And have no fellowship with the unfruitful works of darkness, but rather reprove them."
—Ephesians 5:11

Believers, have a solemn responsibility to prove, examine or judge what will prosper or fare well in the sight of the Lord (Ephesians 5:10). Paul admonishes us to scrutinize and carefully investigate whether a thing is genuine or not. Our aim is to strive to please God by doing what He deems worthy.

When this objective is fully embraced, we are instructed to **absolutely** refuse to partake of, partner, fellowship or be united with barren things (by work, act or deed). When we align ourselves with unfruitful works, we pervert the divine power of God in u enabling it to be snatched away or used by the enemy, as was the case with Balaam, a former prophet of God led astray by his love of money.

If we continue on this course, eventually we'll become puffed up in our hearts. Thus diminishing our usefulness to the Kingdom of God. And eventually we will fall from our elevated position as fruitful spiritual sons of God as Satan did. We would have successfully removed ourselves from among the living, because these dead works will become our own elected office, which is rebellious, temporal and oppositional to the cause of God which inevitably leads to ruin and death.

Unprofitable undertakings that occupy our time and energies darken our spiritual vision. They spread thick dark clouds of error around us, eventually cloaking us in the shadow of death from which we've been redeemed. This is why Paul strongly admonishes us to *absolutely* deny any opportunity for unity with dead works.

We are to judge all things and to be willing to reprove dead enterprises or activities. We are to expose, convict, correct, punish, chasten, call into account, demand an explanation, show one's fault, and or bring the matter into the light.

> *"But he that is spiritual judgeth all things, yet he himself is judged of no man."*
> —1 Corinthians 2:15

We have a duty to walk uprightly before God in order to produce profitable fruit. Furthermore, we are entrusted to be watchman for our brother. If we see that, he is in danger of ceasing to exist or remaining among the spiritually living, we're to call him into account and request an explanation in love.

As children of light, we are to walk in the light of God and to assist and encourage our brother to do the same.

> *"Be ye not unequally yoked together with unbelievers: for what fellowship hath righteousness with unrighteousness? and what communion hath light with darkness?"*
> —1 Corinthians 6:14

"If we say that we have fellowship with him, and walk in darkness, we lie, and do not the truth:"

—1 John 1:6

Therefore, as light bearers we are to be producers of fruitful works that lead to bright eyes and sound minds in Christ Jesus.

DAY 5

SECRET SINS EXPOSED

Sometimes we fellowship with the works of darkness and don't know it. Engaging in activities, projects, campaigns, or causes which sound good and reasonable but are of no godly value.

Good works are actions please God, advance the kingdom, and are in accordance with His will. Of the many options laid out before us, it is the best choice we could make in a given situation for they line up with the heart and intent of God. They are not self-serving, self-promoting or self-advancing. They testify that we love God and our neighbor as ourselves.

As we walk with God, we'll begin to discern which works are good or evil. We'll perceive whom to work alongside and from whom to separate ourselves. If we are willing to follow God all the way He will lead us along a path we didn't know causing all crooked roads to become straight.

> "And I will bring the blind by a way that they knew not; I will lead them in paths that they have not known: I will make darkness light before them, and crooked things straight. These things will I do unto them, and not forsake them."
>
> —Isaiah 42:16

> "I will go before thee, and make the crooked places straight: I will break in pieces the gates of brass, and cut in sunder the bars of iron:"
>
> —Isaiah 45:2

PRAYER

Dear Lord,

Teach me how to be your trumpet in the earth, speaking out against the works of darkness in my life and cleanse me from all unrighteousness (Isaiah 58:1). Then when my obedience is fulfilled (2 Corinthians 10:6), make me brave and courageous to speak out against the works of darkness I discern around me, in my relationships, home, on my job, in my community, nation, and the church. Amen.

ACTIVITY

Are you ready to go further? Do you want to know what Holy Spirit was really saying in this verse? Take some time to look up the Greek references of today's scripture in your Strong's Concordance or online at the www.blueletterbible.org.

And G2532 have G4790 G0 no G3361 fellowship G4790 with the unfruitful G175 works G2041 of darkness, G4655 but G1161 rather G3123 G2532 reprove G1651 them.

—Ephesians 5:11

DAY 6

DRUNK IN THE NIGHT

"For they that sleep sleep in the night; and they that be drunken are drunken in the night."
—1 Thessalonians 5:7

It is no secret that many choose to let their hair down and explore the delicacies of life in the dark of night. When sleep should be their most pressing concern, they are out in clubs, pubs, visiting other people's spouses, or partaking in other vices. Sadly this is true of believers as well.

Lately, there have been scandal after scandal, which have torn churches, families, and deep relationships apart. Why is it so prevalent? 1 Thessalonians 5:7 gives us a clue. People who normally sleep choose to separate themselves from activity. They join themselves with the activity of going to bed. They willfully move in the direction of rest and slumber. This activity is done at a time when work has ceased (at night).

While sleepers prepare to sleep there is another reality-taking place. It happens at the same time and in addition to the business of sleep. Night signals a time of moral stupidity and darkness it's a time for the weary and drunk to participate in deeds of sin and shame.

The absence of light encourages the wayward to indulge in deeds that would displease the God of Light and Righteousness. Erroneously, many believe that night cloaks them and shields them from the purity of his gaze. It does not!

Night was separated from day as light was from darkness. And we as believers are to separate ourselves from sin and shameful activities which can render us drunk and useless to the purpose of God. Furthermore, drunkenness can cause us to shed the blood of those whose lives depend on our righteous witness to God.

Night was God's gift to us so that our bodies could recover from our toils and labor. Let's use it to honor and glorify God. Why should our lives or activities give glory to the evil one?

DAY 6

SECRET SINS EXPOSED

Insomnia, the inability to fall asleep or stay asleep during the night is a sleep disorder that plagues many. Medications could affect a person's sleep patterns, as can poor life choices.

Too many individuals lack knowledge about the importance of sleep. They stay up watching television, partying, working, or performing some other nighttime activity. But sleep is vital to maintaining good health. It was designed by God to be performed during the night hours after work in the daylight ceases. It allows our bodies to repair itself from the toils and labors of the day.

If you find yourself unable to sleep maybe it's time to have your clock reset by God, *"...for they that sleep, sleep in the night."*

> *"It is vain for you to rise up early, to sit up late, to eat the bread of sorrows: for so he giveth his beloved sleep."*
>
> –Psalms 127:2

PRAYER

Dear Lord,

I repent for my poor choices over the years. I ask You to reset my sleep clock and break me free from insomnia. Enable my body to function and perform the tasks that you have created it to do. I choose to give up nighttime activities, which fail to bring you honor and glory. Let your eyes gaze upon me showing yourself strong in support of me according to your Word (2 Chronicles 16:9a), amen.

ACTIVITY

Do you know what it means to be "drunken?" What happens to your senses or your reasoning skills? Are you in control of yourself or at the mercy of another? Let's look closer at this verse to grasp why God draws a line of distinction between individuals who sleep and those who get "drunken".

> For ^{G1063} they that sleep ^{G2518} sleep ^{G2518} in the night; ^{G3571} and ^{G2532} they that be drunken ^{G3182} are drunken ^{G3184} in the night. ^{G3571}
>
> —1 Thessalonians 5:7

DAY 7

WORKERS OF DARKNESS KNOW NOT THE LIGHT

*"In the dark they dig through houses, which
they had marked for themselves in the daytime:
they know not the light."*
—Job 24:16

In obscurity, many do their labors. They burglarize and infiltrate homes and families with the intent of instituting something else. They involve themselves in the household affairs of others in order to erect a monument (or to change the way the household operates).

This work is a covert operation in which information is gathered during the daytime when things can be seen clearly. A mark or seal is fixed on the house, and it is set aside. The intent is to lock up or stop the progression of righteous living.

They use subtle words or arguments to cause doubt and disbelief. They release suggestions and interjections like arrows to stop spiritual advancement and upward progression. They conjure up new philosophies, theories, ideas, popular views and alternative explanations all to shift our position and to cause us to doubt God and believe another.

Job tells us that those who work in the dark know not the light. They don't perceive the light of God. They don't discern light of prosperity. They don't distinguish between light and darkness (righteousness and wickedness).And they don't learn or have knowledge of light (righteousness).

They lack the glory of God emanating from their faces. Their eyes are blind and darkened. They lack the ability to become bright or to light up (grow in righteousness 2 Corinthians 3:18).

The work of believers should erect a temple or monument of righteousness to God. We are to build in the light of God's glory and grace. We are to help others build by the standard of God. Therefore, our words, actions, counsel, and deeds should be governed and influenced by the light.

> *"And the light shineth in darkness; and the darkness comprehended it not."*
> —John 1:5

If all of creation testifies about God's divine attributes and the heavens declare His glory shouldn't our lives also witness of the goodness of God even more since we are created in His image?

> *"For His invisible attributes, that is, His eternal power and divine nature, have been clearly seen since the creation of the world, being understood through what He has made. As a result, people are without excuse."*
> —Romans 1:20

> *"To the chief Musician, A Psalm of David. The heavens declare the glory of God; and the firmament sheweth his handywork."*
> —Psalms 19:1

Let us keep our light shining so brightly in Christ Jesus so that our lives are not overcome by darkness.

"This then is the message which we have heard of him, and declare unto you, that God is light, and in him is no darkness at all."

—1 John 1:5

DAY 7

SECRET SINS EXPOSED

Envy, covetousness, and greed are sins. Watching with the eyes of a hawk what others have and comparing it to what you don't have, opens the door for darkness to roll in.

One day you may just be looking, and the next you may help yourself to a pen, a disk, or a simple ornament. If we choose to open the door to darkness, we know not the light. Light recognizes darkness. It repels it. It separates itself from it. If we allow ourselves to be joined with darkness, how can we be light?

PRAYER

Dear Lord,

I bless you for the opportunity to live in the light. Help me to repel darkness. Enable me to resist the temptation to grow dim or to walk in moral or ethical shade. Let me follow your example to judge all things according to your standard, choosing always the good. In Jesus name, amen.

ACTIVITY

Do you call sin, sin? Are you willing to call out envy, jealousy, covetousness for what they are? Digging through another's home (life or relationship) is a sinful act whether in thought or deed. It's operating as a thief. Let's look closer at today's verse to understand what Holy Spirit wants to teach us.

In the dark H2822 *they dig through* H2864
houses, H1004 *which they had marked* H2856 *for*
themselves in the daytime: H3119 *they*
know H3045 *not the light.* H216

—Job 24:16

CLEANSE ME FROM SECRET FAULTS

"Who can understand his errors? cleanse thou me from secret faults."

—Psalms 19:12

God alone is able to cleanse us from a sinful nature. He alone can sanctify, purify, deem us innocent or give u new hearts (Ezekiel 36:26 and Psalms 51:10). He does this by his statues (a decree), commandments (a divine rule), ordinance (authoritative order) and judgments (a considered decision) (Psalms 19:8-9). He alone is true and righteous therefore, only He can set the righteous standard for us to follow.

But suppose there was an error in God's commandments, statues or judgments who would be able to discern them? Who has the skill or ability to distinguish between truth and error? Who could perceive them? Who would be equipped to tell God He committed a sin of ignorance? Or that He went astray inadvertently?

No one!

In Psalms 19:12, David makes a strong case for us to trust God even when we do not understand everything. The foundation of our faith is based in the statutes of the Lord. His statutes are right which produce rejoicing in our hearts. His commandments are pure and healing causing once blind eyes to see eternal truths. God's judgments are joined together in truth and righteousness.

The fear of the Lord is pure morally, ceremonially, physically thus causing us to shine brightly before Him as clean and pure vessels. It's not like the sinful fear we have of men. It's a fear founded on his incomparable position as the Existent One. All things exist or come into existence because of Him.

Therefore, we can be confident that God is able to cleanse us from all secret faults, sins or waywardness, emptying us of sinful contaminant, freeing us from their clutches, purging all rebellious roots, and acquitting us from charges of violating His laws (Psalms 51:10). He can cause us to become righteous because we exist in Him through Jesus and it's through Him we become a new creation.

> "Therefore if any man be in Christ, he is a new creature: old things are passed away; behold, all things are become new."
> —2 Corinthians 5:17

> "That they all may be one; as thou, Father, art in me, and I in thee, that they also may be one in us: that the world may believe that thou hast sent me."
> —John 17:21

DAY 8

SECRET SINS EXPOSED

D o you question God's Word? Do you find yourself finding fault with his commandments? Do you judge the soundness of his counsel? Have you ever found yourself being more merciful than righteous? More loving than a truth bearer?

The Corinthian church made this mistake. They tolerated flagrant sin in their midst. Why did they do it? Maybe they didn't know how to address the issue. Or maybe they didn't want to seem judgmental. Or maybe they wanted to correct the brother with love, long suffering and tolerance. Or maybe they just wanted to extend more mercy in the hopes it would cause the brother to change his mind about what he was doing.

Paul however took a different approach.

> *"For I verily, as absent in body, but present in spirit, have judged already, as though I were present, concerning him that hath so done this deed,"*
>
> —1 Corinthians 5:3.

Paul did what God did to Adam, Eve, and the serpent. He judged the matter openly, quickly, and righteously. He called it what it was. He didn't vote on the matter, get a consensus, or angle to see which position would be more favorable to the masses. Paul understood the ways of God and he upheld them.

When we fail to judge things as God does, when we choose to cover sin, when we decide to allow sin in our midst then we are in essence questioning God's standards and rebelling against them. God deals in truth. His standard is righteous. And His expectation is that his children will do the same.

> *But he that is spiritual judgeth all things, yet he himself is judged of no man. For who hath known the mind of the Lord, that he may instruct him? But we have the mind of Christ.*
> —1 Corinthians 2:15-16

PRAYER

Dear Lord,

Thank you for calling me to be one of your sons. Lord help me, to uphold your standard in all that I do and in each decision that I make. Help me to view things the way You do. Analyzing, perceiving, discerning with the mind of Christ and not the mind of a flawed and sinful man (Philippians 2:5 and Romans 12:2). Forgive me for questioning, doubting, and lowering Your standards to accommodate emotionalism, sensualism, human expectations and standards. Enable me to do better each day, selecting the better option to Your honor and glory, amen (Hebrews 5:14).

ACTIVITY

Are you interested in knowing more? Learning more? Then dig deeper into the scripture and discover what the Psalmist is saying in the above verse.

> *Who can understand H995 his errors? H7691 cleanse H5352 thou me from secret H5641 faults.*
> —Psalms 19:12

DAY 9

THE SHAME OF SECRET ACTIVITIES

"For it is a shame even to speak of those things which are done of them in secret."
—Ephesians 5:12

Would you associate with a person who is covered from head to toe with dung? Would you invite that person in to have a cup of tea? Would you take his or her advice on hygiene?

Your answer to those questions is probably a resounding **NO!**

Unfortunately, we might be doing it spiritually and not even know it. On a daily basis, we interact with people who are covered with spiritual dung whether in our work places, schools, charity organizations, neighborhoods and in our churches.

In this letter to the Ephesians, Paul advises them not to be deceived by words devoid of truth. Speeches and sayings are empty when they add no value or benefit to our spiritual growth or advancement (Ephesians 5:6). Paul tells us not to fellowship with them or join yourselves with them. Before we were in darkness but now we walk as children of light.

Paul was desperate to convey the dangers these vain speakers presented to the believers. They are filthy, disfigured (spiritually), they are covered with dishonor and shame. They bathe in it and they are a disgrace because of it. Therefore, neither associate with them nor add to, or participate with what it is that they do.

Why not? Because even to talk about what they do, is a shame. Gossiping, about the things they cause to exist adds to the filth. They do these things in secret to escape notice. Subtlety they sow seeds, planning and concealing what they're working on. They patiently wait to bring it forth on the world stage for all to see.

Woven into the fabric of this chapter, Paul highlight the difference between children of darkness and the children of light. We live by the life giving spirit of God, the one that enables us to exist in the higher rarer atmosphere of the Lord while children of darkness exist in the lower regions guided by the flesh (soulish) nature.

The breath that we breathe is natural to us. We don't plan it. We don't think about it. But we do it automatically. This is how it is for those who walk in darkness and is supposed to be for us who walk in the light of God. We are to take in spiritual things and breathe out spiritual things. If what we release isn't beneficial to the kingdom of God or if it fails to uphold His ordinances then we should refrain from releasing it into the earth or spiritual realm.

However, believers have a solemn responsibility as Paul notes,

"And having in a readiness to revenge all disobedience, when your obedience is fulfilled."
— 2 Corinthians 10:6

We're to be ready to punish all disobedience once we have fulfilled our obedience to God. Therefore, it is clear that we're not to participate in the secret activities of the children of darkness, nor are we to allow them to dim, overshadow, or darken our lights. We however, are to expose these activities to the light through scolding, rebuke, reprimanding, and chastening this will testify that we are of the light.

"And have no fellowship with the unfruitful works of darkness, but rather reprove them.
—Ephesians 5:11

"But all things that are reproved are made manifest by the light: for whatsoever doth make manifest is light."
—Ephesians 5:13

Are you ready to increase your light?

DAY 9

SECRET SINS EXPOSED

Gossip is pervasive in the world and in the church. Low whispers of news that float to the ears of eager listeners. People are thrilled to discover the faults, sins, or poor choices others make. This need or desire is practically everywhere, on the job and in families. It takes up our time on the phone, commands our attention, and is a past time as we eat our meals.

The truth is we should not engage in such a fruitless and worthless pursuits. When we engage in gossip, or recount the shame of the wicked we're spreading spiritual urine. It's water which has been tainted for the expressed purpose of contamination.

> "But Rabshakeh said unto them, Hath my master sent me to thy master, and to thee, to speak these words? hath he not sent me to the men which sit on the wall, that they may eat their own dung, and drink their own piss with you?"
>
> —2 Kings 18:27

Rabshakeh declared the intent of his master in the Syrian language to Eliakim, Shebna and Joah (2 Kings 18:26-27). Then he directly addressed the people giving them the words his master had spoken for them to drink (take in) (2 Kings 18:18-37). The people and the watchmen on the wall listened and took in his words even though they answered him not.

The three representatives tore their clothes as they recounted to King Hezekiah what was said. Listening corrupts. It can destroy faith, dishearten the courageous or cause the righteous light to become dim. Our best safeguard is to guard our ear gates from evil words, monitor our mouths, and be prepared to hear from God (Ecclesiastes 5:1).

> *"So that thou incline thine ear unto wisdom,*
> *and apply thine heart to understanding;"*
> —Proverbs 2:2

> *"Set a watch, O LORD, before my mouth;*
> *keep the door of my lips."*
> —Psalms 141:3

> *"He that keepeth his mouth keepeth his life:*
> *but he that openeth wide his lips shall have*
> *destruction."*
> —Proverbs 13:3

> *"But let your communication be, Yea, yea;*
> *Nay, nay: for whatsoever is more than these*
> *cometh of evil."*
> —Matthew 5:37

> *"Let the words of my mouth, and the*
> *meditation of my heart, be acceptable in thy*
> *sight, O Lord, my strength, and my redeemer."*
> —Psalms 19:14

PRAYER

Dear Lord,

Forgive me for listening to unholy communications. Cleanse me from all unrighteousness in conversation. Help me to be a watchman on the walls guarding my ears and monitoring my tongue. Let the words I speak and the conversations I hear being you glory. My desire is to please you in all things and at all times. This is why I was created and this is the hope of my heart, amen.

ACTIVITY

In order to speak what we have heard or witnessed we first have to take it in. Why is that a bad thing? The key may lie in the meaning for the word shame. If you desire to understand, what Holy Spirit was saying in this verse dig into the Word.

> For _G1063_ it is _G2076_ a shame _G149_ even _G2532_ to speak _G3004_ of those things _G2931_ _G0_ which are done _G1096_ of _G5259_ them _G846_ in secret. _G2931_
> —Ephesians 5:12

DAY 10

WOE UNTO THEM . . . WORKERS OF THE DARK

"Woe unto them that seek deep to hide their counsel from the LORD, and their works are in the dark, and they say, Who seeth us? and who knoweth us?"

—Isaiah 29:15

The painful day is coming. The day that is full of great sorrow. The day when many will cry out in sheer despair. The day when those who work in the dark will be exposed to the light. Woe!

Many believe that they can hide and conceal their activities from the eyes of God. They lurk behind the cloak of darkness. They hold secret meetings. They plot, plan scheme with wicked intentions serving themselves and their sinister agenda. They gather with like-minded individuals consulting, conspiring, advising, and counseling one another waiting for the time when their plans are manifest for the world to see.

Like a play, each one has a role. At the root there is a plot and a climatic ending. Energetically and religiously, they labor to fashion, produce, institute, and order things as they desire. Their intent . . . to keep their activities secret until it appears on the public stage. Their aim to conceal all from preying eyes, subtly weaving a web of confusion, doubt, and compromise in order to enjoin people to them. Their desire to deceive the masses with a twisted and perverse version of God's truth until it is too late for anyone to oppose or stop them. They think no one knows. They believe that no one sees. They may even boast of it.

But Jehovah, the Existent One does see. He does know. He is acquainted with their activities. He observes with his eyes all their doings. He is keeping an accurate record of every thought, intent, deed, plan, and idle word. And He knows that soon the day of great sorrows will come and it will be a woe unto them (Amos 5:18).

As believers, we know nothing escapes the eyes of God. We need not be swept up into the whirlwind of darkness for the Lord has made a way for us to escape the day of his wrath (Psalms 110:5 and Revelation 6:17). There is no reason for us to be deceived. There is no justification for us to be entangled again with darkness.

Let us continue to walk boldly and with confidence in God in his glorious light.

DAY 10

SECRET SINS EXPOSED

No one can hide from the gaze of God. It's foolish to even try. Men may be blind but God is not. Are there things that you have hidden from family, friends, brethren? If you have there's only one option for you, if you're a child of light: confession and repentance.

> *If we confess our sins, he is faithful and just to forgive us our sins, and to cleanse us from all unrighteousness.*
>
> —1 John 1:9

> *Confess your faults one to another, and pray one for another, that ye may be healed. The effectual fervent prayer of a righteous man availeth much.*
>
> —James 5:16

Remember God sent Jesus in order for us to know Him. Our objective is to be known (existing in the light). If we desire to hide then the spirit of God is not in us. For God exists in the light and there's no darkness in Him (1 John 1:5, Matthew 5:14-16, and Luke 11:33).

PRAYER

Dear Lord,

Forgive me for hiding in the dark out of fear, shame, or wrong motives. Create in me a clean heart and renew a righteous spirit within me

(Psalms 51:10). Lord I confess that I have not lived, as I ought. And I have done what was displeasing in your sight. Provide for me the opportunity to make things right with those I have wronged. Purify my heart, motives, desires and mind so it may be healed, in Jesus name I pray, amen (Psalms 139:23-24 and Psalms 51:7-15).

ACTIVITY

Why do people seek to hide and lurk in the dark? Does it provide false safety? Or does it make it easier to escape detection. Why does the prophet Isaiah say woe to them that seek deep to hide? If you're curious about this, then here's your opportunity to learn more.

> *Woe* <u>H1945</u> *unto them that seek deep* <u>H6009</u> *to hide* <u>H5641</u> *their counsel* <u>H6098</u> *from the LORD,* <u>H3068</u> *and their works* <u>H4639</u> *are in the dark,* <u>H4285</u> *and they say,* <u>H559</u> *Who seeth* <u>H7200</u> *us? and who knoweth* <u>H3045</u> *us?*
>
> —Isaiah 29:15

DAY 11

ANCIENT ACTIVITES IN THE DARK

"Then said he unto me, Son of man, hast thou seen what the ancients of the house of Israel do in the dark, every man in the chambers of his imagery? for they say, The LORD seeth us not; the LORD hath forsaken the earth."
—Ezekiel 8:12

Jehovah is an exposer of concealed acts. Ezekiel 8:12 demonstrates that God will reveal our hidden sins to others if we persist on doing what is displeasing in his sight. Israel's old men, the ones with authority proudly worshipped idols and indulged in vain imaginations in secret rooms.

They gave the sacred place in their hearts to these abominations, arrogantly boasting that the Lord didn't perceive, discern, or observe their acts. They even conjured a lie, that God had forsaken the whole earth and the inhabitants of the land.

We're told that every man without exception, whether a great man, servant, or husband each one individually and collectively participated in this dark activity. These men were not boys, or youths, their chins hung down, and they showed the signs of age, yet they acted foolishly and without shame.

Ezekiel was summoned by God to observe, perceive, and consider what his brethren were doing. He was alerted to their secret sins. God showed him what took place in the dark in order to correct the ancients of Israel. God turned on a lantern so that they would see their actions for what it was *sin.* His desire was for them to turn from sinful ways and repent (Matthew 18:15-17).

Furthermore, God addressed several critical facts; firstly, that He saw what they were doing. Secondly, nothing was hidden from Him and He had not abandoned the earth or the inhabitants of the land. Thirdly, that He was an exposer, for He caused Ezekiel to see the elders for who and what they were.

Ezekiel was God's witness, therefore the matter was firmly established.

> "At the mouth of two witnesses, or three witnesses, shall he that is worthy of death be put to death; but at the mouth of one witness he shall not be put to death."
> —Deut. 17:6

> "One witness shall not rise up against a man for any iniquity, or for any sin, in any sin that he sinneth: at the mouth of two witnesses, or at the mouth of three witnesses, shall the matter be established."
> —Deut. 19:15

God follows the same standard He instructs us to follow if there is an offense or sin. We are to inform the person, approach him again with a witness, and finally take the matter to the church. If he hears, then we have gained a brother if not we are to cut him off.

> "Moreover if thy brother shall trespass against thee, go and tell him his fault between thee and him alone: if he shall hear thee, thou hast gained thy brother. But if he will not hear thee, then take with thee one or two more, that in the mouth of two or three witnesses every word may be established. And if he shall neglect to hear

them, tell it unto the church: but if he neglect to hear the church, let him be unto thee as an heathen man and a publican."
—Matthew 18:15-17

God isn't a respecter of persons. What He did for the ancients of Israel He will do for us and the standard He follows is the one laid out for us. Let's expose our secret sins to the light before God has to do it for us!

Search me, O God, and know my heart: try me, and know my thoughts: And see if there be any wicked way in me, and lead me in the way everlasting.
—Ps. 139:23-24

DAY 11

SECRET SINS EXPOSED

Today's devotional verse is rather sobering. Just because a person has authority or has lived a long time (is aged) doesn't mean that he is wise or righteous. We can learn a lot from the elderly, good things as well as bad. It's our responsibility to judge all things, discern the good from the evil and then choose the good, or the better option (Galatians 6:9, 1 Peter 3:9, and Romans 12:17-21).

The ancients committed secret sins. They passed it down until others were ensnared. They lied on God to justify their sin. If you know the right, you're responsible to do it. If you fail, the consequences might be more than you' re willing to pay.

> *"And when the prophet that brought him back from the way heard thereof, he said, It is the man of God, who was disobedient unto the word of the LORD: therefore the LORD hath delivered him unto the lion, which hath torn him, and slain him, according to the word of the LORD, which he spake unto him."*
> —1 Kings 13:26

The young prophet lost his life because he listened to the words of an elder prophet in disobedience to God. Are you willing to pay the same price?

PRAYER

Dear Lord,

Help me to obey your voice alone (Deuteronomy 28:1, 30:10 and 27:10) Increase my discernment. Help me to perceive Your will in each situation. Lord grow me in the ways of confidence in You and eliminate all fear from my life (1 John 4:17-18, 2 Timothy 1:7, and Psalms 119:39). Forgive me where I have obeyed the voice of another including my own. I want to be like Jesus doing what You direct me to do and listening to the words that You speak to me through Your Spirit (John 5:19, John 16:13, Proverbs 16:9, Psalms 32:8, and Proverbs 3:6).

ACTIVITY

When God watches you in the dark, what does He observe you doing? Invest some time today to seek more understanding from God as you dive into Ezekiel 8:12.

> Then said *H559* he unto me, Son *H1121* of man, *H120* hast thou seen *H7200* what the ancients *H2205* of the house *H1004* of Israel *H3478* do *H6213* in the dark, *H2822* every man *H376* in the chambers *H2315* of his imagery? *H4906* for they say, *H559* The LORD *H3068* seeth *H7200* us not; the LORD *H3068* hath forsaken *H5800* the earth. *H776*

—Ezekiel 8:12

EVIL DOERS HATE THE LIGHT OF REPROOF

"For every one that doeth evil hateth the light, neither cometh to the light, lest his deeds should be reproved."

—John 3:20

How do you respond to correction? What is your first impulse when your boss refutes something you've said? What are your thoughts when your brother or sister in Christ finds fault with something that you have done? Are you pleased when God exposes your sin in the light of His Word?

In our society today, many people hate correction. John 3:20 spells out the reason this is so. Individuals who are ethically bankrupt, who enjoy worthless activities, who are of no account to the kingdom of God detest moral and spiritual truth. They hate to be judged, forced to give an account, or obliged to give an explanation.

Evil doers don't just hate light, they loathe being near light. Light has the ability to cause them to be seen for who and what they are, disobedient rebels.

The world cannot hate you; but me it hateth, because I testify of it, that the works thereof are evil.

—John 7:7

When we as believers operate in the light we are lamps for Christ and evil doers will hate us, because we prevent them from having a cloke (pretext) for their sin.

> *If the world hate you, ye know that it hated me before it hated you. If you belonged to the world, it would love you as its own. As it is, you do not belong to the world, but I have chosen you out of the world. That is why the world hates you.*
>
> —John 15:18-19

> *If I had not come and spoken unto them, they had not had sin: but now they have no cloke for their sin.*
>
> —John 15:22

Do you love light? Do you yearn to be near it? Do you celebrate and thank God when He corrects you?

> *For whom the Lord loveth he chasteneth, and scourgeth every son whom he receiveth.*
>
> —Hebrews 12:6

> *For whom the LORD loveth he correcteth; even as a father the son in whom he delighteth.*
>
> —Proverbs 3:12

True sons of God love the light of reproof. God will help us if we ask.

For every one that asketh receiveth; and he that seeketh findeth; and to him that knocketh it shall be opened.

—Matthew 7:7

DAY 12

SECRET SINS EXPOSED

In life, there are people we're drawn to like magnets and others that repel us like the smell of compost. Or is it because those people are good, that we are drawn to them? Is it that the others are wicked why we are repelled?

There were many who found Christ repulsive. The light He emitted offended the eyes of those who loved the dark. Sometimes we get it wrong. Those we like could be dangerous to our spiritual health, while the ones who repulse us may be what we need to prosper, grow or regain our spiritual vitality.

We should endeavor to walk with those who purpose to follow the will of God (Amos 3:3).

PRAYER

Dear Lord,

Thank you for your wisdom and discernment. Help me to be drawn to Your Word and other children of light. Let us be in one accord and led by Your spirit. Weed out those who cause dimness in my life. Separate me from those who hate light and reproof. Crown me with Your glory I pray, amen (Psalms 8:5 and 2 Corinthians 3:18).

ACTIVITY

You're a lover of light, therefore you hate evil and desire to avoid the dark. As you examine the Word of God, you increase the light in your life. Enjoy the journey into brighter light.

For G1063 every one G3956 that doeth G4238 evil G5337 hateth G3404 the light, G5457 neither G2532 G3756 cometh G2064 to G4314 the light, G5457 lest G3363 his G846 deeds G2041 should be reproved. G1651

—*John 3:20*

DAY 13

MURDERING THEIVES

"The murderer rising with the light killeth the poor and needy, and in the night is as a thief."
—Job 24:14

There's an inherent danger in being a worker of darkness (Psalms 37:2). It doesn't change us overnight turning us into evil personified, but it does cause us to change slowly, methodically and deliberately.

If we continue, walking on the *dark side* and feasting at the banquet table of the enemy we'll inevitably grow dark. Things that we once had an aversion to will start to look appealing, attractive, and less sinful (Romans 1:22-32). The defining line between right and wrong will no longer be clear to us.

Helping those who are afflicted or weak would cease to be a top priority; rather they will be considered expendable or a means to an end. We may believe that we're immune to such depraved actions or thoughts but if David, a man after God's own heart succumbed to it, do we stand a chance if we flirt with the foul pleasures of darkness?

"Woe to them that devise iniquity, and work evil upon their beds! when the morning is light, they practice it, because it is in the power of their hand."
—Micah 2:1

Once we become workers of darkness, our thinking becomes dark and we no longer hide our acts or intentions under the cloak of the night light. We will no longer be able to tell the difference between night and day, good and evil, or right and wrong. Therefore, we will indulge in secret sins of gossip, deceit, debate envy, covetousness, wickedness, fornication, unrighteousness, boasting, disobedience, evil, unnatural affections, and being without mercy and in some cases committing murder in the light of day (Romans 1:29-32). Our acts will be premeditated, vengeful, bent on assassinating and crushing people into pieces.

We all have encountered individuals who try to crush others with their power, position, influence or words. They try to assassinate them with their arrows of gossip. Or actively campaign to kill any advancement due to their hidden sins of unforgiveness, envy, jealousy, or covetousness. They are determined to prevent the person from prospering.

In the still of the night, long after the sun has gone down they secretly steal, what the person needs the most, deliverance from oppression and abuse. Instead of leading them into the light, they find ways to rob them of an opportunity for light, hope, or salvation making their situation more wretched by denying them what they long for . . . to be set free.

How?

By keeping silent or not sharing godly counsel.

"He devises mischief upon his bed; he sets himself in a way that is not good; he abhors not evil."
                                        —Psalms 36:4

As spiritual beings in Christ Jesus we are to be our brother's keeper, gently restoring him with correction, love and support (Galatians 6:1-2).

"Moreover if thy brother shall trespass against thee, go and tell him his fault between thee and

him alone: if he shall hear thee, thou hast gained thy brother."
—Matthew 18:15

If he refuses then Paul outlines in 1 Corinthians 5 what believers should do in order to save his soul.

"To deliver such an one unto Satan for the destruction of the flesh, that the spirit may be saved in the day of the Lord Jesus."
—1 Corinthians 5:5

Secret sins desire to make themselves known. As seeds, they grow unnoticed underground, patiently waiting for the day when they will burst through the resistance, and emerge on the world stage, basking in the light, visible for all to see and know exactly who and what they are— murdering thieves (takers of life Genesis 2:17).

"You shall know them by their fruits. Do men gather grapes of thorns, or figs of thistles?"

—Matthew 7:16

What does your fruit say about you?

DAY 13

SECRET SINS EXPOSED

It's a challenge at times to have the right heart in every situation. Sometimes the wrongs people do to us can cause us to operate in an unrighteous fashion. At other times, blindness to our own ambitions or objectives can conceal the path of righteousness; then at other times the cravings of our hearts can cause us to take advantage of those we should help.

No matter what the reason, we are not to be murderers but deliverers. We are not to be thieves but givers. We were chosen to be a blessing in the earth (Genesis 22:18) as we consent to the trying of your faith.

"Bless them that curse you, and pray for them which despitefully use you."
—Luke 6:28

"My brethren, count it all joy when ye fall into divers temptations; Knowing this, that the trying of your faith worketh patience. But let patience have her perfect work, that ye may be perfect and entire, wanting nothing."
—James 1:2-4

And if judgment is needed we are to judge, for in so doing we demonstrate the love of God, because it opens a door of opportunity for repentance.

For whom the LORD loveth he correcteth; even as a father the son in whom he delighteth.
—Proverbs 3:12

As many as I love, I rebuke and chasten: be zealous therefore, and repent.
—Revelation 3:19

For whom the Lord loveth he chasteneth, and scourgeth every son whom he receiveth.
—Hebrews 12:6

PRAYER

Dear Lord,

Please forgive me where in I have hurt others, or robbed them of an opportunity to repent from their sins. Where I have watched them go down the path of destruction and kept my mouth shut. If I have wronged my fellow man or oppressed them, please forgive me. Lord help me to be a life giver as I share Your Word with others. Help me to be a gift giver as I poor out the blessings, which You have provided for those You call.

"And if the house be worthy, let your peace come upon it: but if it be not worthy, let your peace return to you."
—Matthew 10:13

Not rendering evil for evil, or railing for railing: but contrariwise blessing; knowing that ye are thereunto called, that ye should inherit a blessing.
—1 Peter 3:9

ACTIVITY

What has changed for the murderer why does he now conduct his business in the light of day? Why does he go after the poor and needy? Does this verse expose the progression of evil of wickedness? Examine the verse closer with the help of Holy Spirit and let Him reveal the hidden truths.

> *"The murderer* H7523 *rising* H6965 *with the light* H216 *killeth* H6991 *the poor* H6041 *and needy,* H34 *and in the night* H3915 *is as a thief.* H1590 *"*

—Job 24:14

DAY 14

SHEW THYSELF TO THE WORLD

"For there is no man that doeth any thing in secret, and he himself seeketh to be known openly. If thou do these things, shew thyself to the world."

—John 7:4

Masks, we've all worn them at some point in our lives whether for Halloween, or at a masquerade ball, or as part of a play. They're the type of disguise that comes off after the event has passed. But people wear other kinds of masks, the ones which are veiled behind a smile, or flowery words, hiding their true intentions, feelings, thoughts or their self.

On the surface, advice given to Jesus by his brethren in John 7:4, appears sound and wise. Reveal yourself to others they said. Make yourself known, after all this is why you came. Give others the opportunity to witness your great miracles.

Jesus however didn't follow their counsel because His time table was determined by God and not men.

Why did they give Him this advice? What did they hope to gain? Were they interested in advancing God's agenda or their own? Did they desire to do what was best for Jesus or for themselves? What was lurking behind their masks?

As believers, we need to be in tune with the agenda of God. Many will give advice which sounds wise but goes against God's plan for our lives. The counsel could be sincere, but may not necessarily biblically or spiritually sound. God will ensure that his plans in our lives are not derailed if we follow his timeline. He alone should decide when the right time is for us to *shew ourselves to the world.*

When we force the issue, our light is diminished; it's not as brilliant as it ought to be. He will cause our light to pierce through the darkness and meet the eyes of on-lookers. He will ensure that the teachings we share are sound, true and righteous bringing Him the glory and honor He deserves. God will ensure that our lives are ornaments befitting the King of Kings.

When we follow our own counsel or the advice of others, we may birth things prematurely. Premature birth (in the natural) could lead to many complications the same is true for premature spiritual birth.

In the natural, a premature baby could develop breathing disorders, heart and brain problems, temperature control abnormalities, metabolism issues, blood, and immune system problems. The same is true for spiritually premature babies. The air sought after would be the lower denser air of earthliness, the flesh. Their heart's desire would be earthly and temporal not kingdom or God centered.

Our minds, which should be like that of Christ, would not be fully developed resulting in poor decisions and an inability to decipher between good and evil. Or they could remain lukewarm or cold rather than hot or boiling for God because of temperature issues. Due to metabolism complications they could lack the energy to go the full distance and complete the race. If the spiritual immune system is compromised, susceptibility to corruption or infection by false doctrines or temptations could result.

Problems with our natural blood cells could cause us to put our faith in other things beside the blood of Jesus and the promises of God when facing challenges in our lives (Leviticus 17:11).

Our development as spiritual sons of God should be fed by the Word of God and governed and directed by Holy Spirit.

> *"As newborn babes, desire the sincere milk of the word, that ye may grow thereby: If so be ye have tasted that the Lord is gracious."*
> —1 Peter 2:3

We will know when the time comes to shew ourselves to the world for God will lead us.

> *"For as many as are led by the Spirit of God, they are the sons of God."*
> —Romans 8:14

DAY 14

SECRET SINS EXPOSED

Zealousness is often an asset but there are times when it could cause us to act rashly and prematurely. Zealousness could cause us to neglect inquiring of the Lord. In 2 Samuel 7:8-17, we learn of David's desired to build a temple for the Lord. He discussed his intent with the prophet Nathan who approved it. Nathan neglected to seek God impute first and was ordered to correct his error. The prophet Elijah also failed to seek God's counsel when Jezebel threatened to kill him (1 Kings 19:1-4).

God wants us to be full of righteous jealousy for things that are important to Him, but He also wants us to seek His counsel before we act. We should ask God for wisdom in every situation for He has it waiting in His storehouse for us and He has promised to pour it out liberally for us (James 1:5).

"He layeth up sound wisdom for the righteous: he is a buckler to them that walk uprightly. He keepeth the paths of judgment, and preserveth the way of his saints. Then shalt thou understand righteousness, and judgment, and equity; yea, every good path. When wisdom entereth into thine heart, and knowledge is pleasant unto thy soul;"
—Proverbs 2:7-10

Are you willing to ask (Luke 11:9)? Are you willing to seek (Matthew 6:33)? Are you willing to wait (Psalms 27:14)? Are you willing to change your mind and admit that you acted hastily? If you are then He will keep you by the soundness of His wisdom. He will preserve your ways and transform your heart by the knowledge of who He is.

PRAYER

Dear Lord,

Give me good sense. Help me to know what is right just and fair. Lead me on the right course every time. Fill my heart with wisdom and give me the joy of knowing You intimately. Keep me safe by understanding and may Your plans for my life watch over me. Reveal me to the world when You deem it the right time. And may I grow in patience waiting with the joy of the Lord as my strength (Psalms 28:7 and Nehemiah 8:10). Amen (based on Proverbs 2:10-11 NIV).

ACTIVITY

Why did these men give Jesus the counsel they did? And why didn't He listen to them? Are there people who you should not listen to? How would you know? Why not find out by examining this verse a little closer.

> *For* G1063 *there is no man* G3762 *that doeth* G4160 *any thing* G5100 *in* G1722 *secret,* G2927 *and* G2532 *he himself* G846 *seeketh* G2212 *to be* G1511 *known openly.* G1722 G3954 *If* G1487 *thou do* G4160 *these things,* G5023 *shew* G5319 *thyself* G4572 *to the world.* G2889
>
> —John 7:4

DAY 15

ALL WILL BE MANIFESTED

"For there is nothing hid, which shall not be manifested; neither was any thing kept secret, but that it should come abroad."

—Mark 4:22

When it comes to the activities of men or occurrences in history, absolutely nothing will remain hidden. Mark issues an absolute denial that secret things will or could remain concealed. Those who believe that tiny sins or indiscretions will not come to light choose to believe a lie rather than **truth**.

Mark 4:22 states that *all* will be manifest. It will be evident, plain to see, thoroughly understood, and made apparent. At the root of this scripture is the understanding that secret things will be brought into the light. God will cause light to shine upon our activities causing us to be seen for who and what we are.

At that time, we will fully understand what moral and spiritual truth is. On that day when our lives, thoughts, spiritual purity or lack thereof are publicly displayed there will be no place to hide.

This is not a new concept. No one will escape judgment, even Satan will be exposed and judged for who and what he is (Revelation 20:7-10). God is not a respecter of persons or creatures, He doesn't play favorites. He judges by one standard. Each of us will be judged based on what is written in the books that will open before Christ (Revelation 20:11-15).

If we expose our secret sins to the light of God now, and turn from the works of darkness, we are indeed children of light thus assuring that our names will be in the book of life. Our aim is to work toward the day when like Christ we can declare, *"… for the prince of this world cometh, and hath nothing in me"* John 14:30b.

"This then is the message which we have heard of him, and declare unto you, that God is light, and in him is no darkness at all."

—1 John 1:5

Our aim is to be like our Father and Brother Jesus let no darkness be in us.

DAY 15

SECRET SINS EXPOSED

Many people live in fear of discovery. A spouse may be afraid that if his or her partner knew the real him or her that they would leave. Politicians live with the knowledge that one wrong act exposed could spell the end of their political aspirations. Pastors worry that a revealed indiscretion could cost them the pulpit and the loss of their followers.

These things shouldn't cause us to be fearful, to worry, or to have anxiety. What can man do to us? Can they put us in hell? Can they tell us we cannot enter the kingdom of God? Can they cast us into outer darkness? No, they can't.

Can they reveal every sinful thing we've ever done with our bodies? Can they list every idle word we have spoken with our mouth? Can they display before the public every foul thought? No, they can't.

But Christ can and He will. This is why we are called to work out our salvation with fear and trembling (Philippians 2:12). Men can't protect us nor can they save us, that task was given to Christ Jesus alone. It's our responsibility as believers to allow the Spirit of God to keep us on the path we have chosen.

PRAYER

Dear Lord,

Help me to live a life of exposure existing in the light. Telling all, admitting all, and seeking to be myself true before You. Help me to overcome all temptations and secret sin. Help me to call a lie a lie (Proverbs 6:16-19). Let my yea be yea and my nay be nay (Matthew 5:37). I desire to sow well so I can reap well in the abundance of Christ Jesus. Forgive all former transgressions known and unknown. Bless me so that as of this day, I walk in the light confident that I can overcome every secret sin. Amen.

ACTIVITY

Do you know what will become manifest on that day when all is revealed? Is it seared in your heart? Imprinted in your mind? If not take time to ask God to help you to grasp the fullness of Mark 4:22. Ask Him to write it upon the table of your heart (Proverbs 7:3).

> *For* G1063 *there is* G2076 *nothing* G3756 *hid,* G2927 G5100 *which* G3739 *shall* G5319 G0 *not* G3362 *be manifested;* G5319 *neither* G3761 *was any thing kept* G1096 *secret,* G614 *but* G235 *that* G2443 *it should come* G2064 *abroad.* G1519 G5318

—Mark 4:22

CONCLUSION

As believers, we are charged with a solemn task. God will not do it for us, though He will strongly support us if we choose to do it (2 Chronicles 16:9). We have to choose to live in the light our existence as sons of God demands that we love light, desire to be near the light, and that we are bearers of light (John 1:5, Acts 17:11, and 1 John 1:5).

If we don't like light, prefer darkness, dabble in secret sins, or occasionally stroll in the shadows then we are breaking our covenant vows to God. God has made a way for us to follow His example, it's not an impossible task for Christ did it. God has even stacked the deck in our favor by sending Holy Spirit to reside with us on the earth. But even more importantly the entire Godhead exists and lives in us if we choose to allow them to help us clean house.

"Jesus answered and said unto him, If a man love me, he will keep my words: and my Father will love him, and we will come unto him, and make our abode with him."
—John 14:23

"Or else how can one enter into a strong man's house, and spoil his goods, except he first bind the strong man? and then he will spoil his house."
—Matthew 12:29

"He that committeth sin is of the devil; for the devil sinneth from the beginning. For this purpose the Son of God was manifested, that he might destroy the works of the devil."
—1 John 3:8

Christ alone is the true strongman. He came to destroy the works of the devil and He did, for Satan was condemned (John 12:30-31 and John 16:10-11). When we allow Christ to be Lord of our lives He will continue to manifest His power by breaking, destroying, shaking, burning, eliminating and delivering us from the works of the devil and from the darkness that dwells within (Mark 7:15, 20) and around us (Romans 7:21). As we believe and operate with the authority Christ has given us, we too will become strongmen able to destroy the works of the devil (Luke 10:19) and help others to do the same.

May God continue to bless you as you walk deeper into the light of His presence.

www.ingramcontent.com/pod-product-compliance
Lightning Source LLC
Chambersburg PA
CBHW061154040426
42445CB00013B/1683